COVER TO COVER

The Lord's Prayer

PRAYING JESUS' WAY

CWR

Selwyn Hughes
with Ian Sewter

Copyright © CWR 2008

Published 2008 by CWR, Waverley Abbey House, Waverley Lane, Farnham,
Surrey GU9 8EP, UK. Registered Charity No. 294387.
Registered Limited Company No. 1990308.
Reprinted 2010, 2011, 2013.

Text taken from *Every Day with Jesus, The Lord's Prayer*, July/August 1983 by
Selwyn Hughes. Adaptation and additional material by Ian Sewter.

All rights reserved. No part of this publication may be reproduced, stored in
a retrieval system, or transmitted, in any form or by any means, electronic,
mechanical, photocopying, recording or otherwise, without the prior permission
in writing of CWR.

See back of book for list of National Distributors.

Unless otherwise indicated, all Scripture references are from the Holy Bible:
New International Version (NIV), copyright © 1973, 1978, 1984 by the
International Bible Society.

Other quotations are marked: Amp: The Amplified Bible Old Testament,
copyright © 1965, 1987 by the Zondervan Corporation. The Amplified New
Testament, copyright © 1958 by the Lockman Foundation. Used by permission.
TLB: *The Living Bible*, copyright © 1971, 1994, Tyndale House Publishers.
Message: Scripture taken from *The Message*. Copyright © 1993, 1994, 1995, 1996,
2000, 2001, 2002. Used by permission of NavPress Publishing Group. NLT:
From the *Holy Bible*, New Living Translation, copyright © 1996, 2004. Used by
permission of Tyndale House Publishers, Inc., Wheaton, Illinois 60189. All rights
reserved. AV: The Authorised Version. Moffatt: *The Moffatt Translation of the
Bible*, copyright © 1987, Hodder & Stoughton.

Concept development, editing, design and production by CWR
Cover image: istockphoto and Stockxpert
Printed in the UK by Page Brothers

ISBN: 978-1-85345-460-8

Contents

5   Introduction

9   Week 1
Father in Heaven

15   Week 2
Honouring God's Name

21   Week 3
God's Kingdom Come

27   Week 4
God's Will be Done

33   Week 5
Our Daily Needs

39   Week 6
The Freedom of Forgiveness

45   Week 7
Overcoming Evil and Seeing God's Glory

51   Leader's Notes

Introduction

In this study we embark upon an in-depth examination of one of the most precious passages in the whole of the New Testament – the Lord's Prayer. These words of Jesus, seemingly so simple, encompass every conceivable element in prayer and reduce it to a clearly understood pattern. In the short compass of sixty-six words, the Master presents a model of praying that touches on every major aspect of prayer. No set of theological volumes, no sermon, no series of writings could ever capture the fullness of all that prayer is as does this simple yet profound model. The more we understand this model, and the more we pray in line with it, the more powerful and productive our prayer life will become.

All communication with God begins with prayer, and because this communication is so important, the enemy seeks to disrupt it. This is why we face the necessity to constantly refocus our thinking on the subject, and seek to deepen and enhance our prowess in the art of prayer. If the Lord's Prayer sets the standard for all praying, then we must lay our praying alongside His pattern in order that our prayers might become more and more like His.

Some Christians think that prayer consists solely of reciting the words of the Lord's Prayer but, as the great preacher C.H. Spurgeon once said, 'To recite the Lord's Prayer and believe that you have then prayed is the height of foolishness.' This does not mean, of course, that there is no spiritual value in reciting it. I would not want to deprive Christian congregations of the pleasure and joy of reciting together the Lord's Prayer, but I do want to encourage them to view it as a departure point rather than an arrival platform. If Jesus advised His disciples not to use 'vain repetitions, as the heathen do', would He then immediately follow it by giving us a prayer to simply recite? If we are to obtain the greatest value from the Lord's Prayer, then we must view it as a skeleton on which we have to put flesh. If you view these words, not merely as something to recite, but as an outline from which you must work your way when praying, no matter what you are praying about, then you will experience a growing confidence that you are praying the way Jesus taught. You see, it's one thing to recite a prayer: it's another thing to know how to pray.

Look at the first word with which the prayer begins – 'Our'. That first word determines the very nature of the Christian faith. Suppose it had begun 'My'? Instead of our faith being 'our'-centred it would have been 'my'-centred – and that would have started us off wrongly. In the field of prayer, as in many other fields, to start wrongly is to finish wrongly. The word 'our' involves a shifting of emphasis from me to the Father, and to my brothers and sisters in the kingdom. It implies a renunciation – a renunciation of myself. We see something similar in the first words of the Beatitudes: 'Blessed are the poor in spirit [the renounced in spirit] for theirs is the kingdom of heaven' (Matt. 5:3). All the resources of the kingdom belong to the renounced in spirit. So, in the first word of the Lord's Prayer, we find an implied demand that we adopt an attitude of self-surrender – surrender to the Father, and to His interests, and the interests of others in His kingdom. If we do this, then everything opens to us. If not, then everything is closed. The rest of the Lord's Prayer has no meaning, and dies if the 'Our' is not alive. And what does this mean for the person using Jesus' model of prayer? It means that the 'Our' must stretch beyond our own fellowship, local church or denomination to include the whole family of God – everywhere. We will never get very far in prayer unless we come to it prepared to sacrifice self-interest, and willing to merge into God's greater plan for the whole. An unknown author put it this way:

I cannot say 'our' if I live only for myself. I cannot say, 'Father' if I do not try to act like His child. I cannot say, 'who art in heaven' if I am laying up no treasure there. I cannot say, 'hallowed be thy name' if I am not striving for holiness. I cannot say, 'Thy kingdom come' if I am not doing all in my power to hasten that event. I cannot say, 'give us this day our daily bread' if I am dishonest, or seeking something for nothing. I cannot say, 'forgive us our trespasses' if I bear a grudge against another. I cannot say, 'lead us not into temptation' if I deliberately place myself in its path. I cannot say, 'deliver us from evil' if I do not put on the armour of God. I cannot say, 'thine is the kingdom and the power and the glory' if I do not give the King the loyalty due to Him from a faithful subject. And I cannot say, 'for ever' if the horizon of my life is bounded completely by time.

The whole thrust of the Lord's Prayer is that when we give God His rightful place, He gives us our rightful place. But not before.

WEEK 1

Father in Heaven

Opening Icebreaker

Try to list as many qualities as you can of a good father, and then pray the Lord's Prayer together if you are in a group, or out loud if you are on your own.

Bible Readings

- Isaiah 40:18–31
- Luke 6:35–36
- Luke 11:1–12
- Luke 15:11–32
- Romans 8:14–17

Opening Our Eyes

Prayer should always begin with the recognition that God is our Father, but it is not enough that we address God as 'Father' simply by saying the word with our lips. We must understand the nature of God's fatherhood, for if we don't, then we will never be able to pray the way Jesus laid down for us. No one can rise higher in his prayer life than his concept of God. If you do not hold in your heart a picture of God as He really is, then your prayers will be short-circuited, and, like electricity when it has nowhere else to go, will run into the earth.

Jesus shows us in the first sentence of His prayer pattern that true prayer must begin with a concept of God as Father. The term 'Father' answers all the philosophical questions about the nature of God. A father is a person, therefore God is not an invisible force behind the machinery of the universe. A father is able to hear, therefore God is not an impersonal being, aloof from all our troubles and trials. And, above all, a father is predisposed, by reason of his familial relationship, to give careful attention to what his child says. When we pray, then, to the Father, we must hold in our minds the picture of our eternal Creator as a Being who has a father's heart, a father's love and a father's strength. Time and time again, I have watched Christians struggle over this issue. They ask God for things which in their intellects they know are right and proper, yet they fail to get answers to their prayers because, deep down in their hearts, they have a doubt about His willingness to respond to them. This is why, if we are to learn to pray the Jesus way, we must seek to develop a clear understanding of the fatherhood of God.

So how can we gain a picture of God's fatherhood that is true to reality? We do it by focusing upon Jesus. He is the expression of the Father in human form. In John 14:9 Jesus explained that, 'Anyone who has seen me has seen the Father.' If you want to know what God is like as a Father, then gaze at Jesus. He drives the mists and misconceptions from around the Deity, and shows us that the heart that throbs at the back of the universe is like His heart – a sacrificial heart overflowing with unconditional love.

Before we can pray effectively, we must first be convinced not only of who God is (our Father) but also where God is (in heaven). In other words, the initial focus of our praying should not be on ourselves but on God. Doesn't this reveal at once a fatal weakness in our praying? We come into God's presence and, instead of focusing our gaze upon Him, we focus it on our problems and our difficulties, which serve, in turn, to increase the awareness of our lack. Perhaps this is the reason why, when praying, we frequently end up more depressed or more frustrated than when we began. This is one of the greatest lessons we can learn about prayer – the initial focus must be upon God. I believe that Jesus, in using the words 'Our Father *in heaven*' (my emphasis), sought to focus our minds, not so much on God's *location*, but rather His *elevation*. In other words, what is impossible for us is possible for Him.

Discussion Starters

1. Is God the Father of all peoples or only of Christians?

2. How may our personal experiences of fathers and authority figures affect our prayer life?

3. Try to identify the thoughts and emotions of the prodigal and his father.

4. How can we know more of what God is like?

5. Why should we refer to heaven in our prayers?

6. Why should we think of heaven in terms of an elevation rather than a location?

7. Why did Jesus begin the prayer, 'Our Father in heaven'?

8. How can we reconcile God's greatness with our smallness?

9. Why may people struggle in prayer?

Personal Application

What goes on in your thoughts and feelings when the word 'father' is mentioned? Some will have positive thoughts and feelings like warmth, love and affection, while others will experience negative feelings such as remoteness, sternness, or even unconcern. For many people, the word 'father' has to be redeemed or amended, because it conjures up memories of unhappy relationships. We must make sure that our concept of the word 'father' is a positive one, for if it isn't, then we will never be able to approach God with the confidence of a trusting child. This is why Christ often taught about the generosity and kindness of God in terms of a good father, even to those who rejected Him and His ways. The parable of the Prodigal Son is just one example of this teaching. In fact, our Father in heaven is even kind to the ungrateful and wicked (Luke 6:35–36) and sends His provision to both the righteous and the unrighteous (Matt. 5:45).

Seeing Jesus in the Scriptures

When we see Jesus in the Scriptures healing the sick, comforting the broken hearted and touching the outcasts, we see the heart of the Father in all He does, for Jesus only did the will of the Father (John 5:19; 6:38; 14:10). Take time to allow the character, words and works of Christ form within you a true perception of God as a loving Father. Jesus Himself often prayed to the Father (eg Matt. 11:25; 26:42; John 17:1,5,11,21,24–25) and so emphasised the real nature of the relationship on which authentic prayer is based.

WEEK | TWO

WEEK 2

Honouring God's Name

Opening Icebreaker

Try to find out the meanings of the names of people in your group. For example, 'John' means 'God's gift'.

Bible Readings

- Exodus 3:13–15
- Exodus 6:2–8
- Psalm 86:5–16
- Psalm 96:1–13
- Matthew 6:9–13

15

Opening Our Eyes

We come now to the next clause in Jesus' pattern of prayer:
'hallowed be your name'. What does it mean to hallow the
name of our loving heavenly Father? To hallow something is
to reverence it, or treat it as sacred. It is derived from a very
important word in the Bible (Greek: *hagiazo*), which means
to venerate, set apart, to make holy. Does this mean that
our veneration of God makes Him holy? No – for nothing
we do can add to His qualities or attributes, and nothing
we do can subtract from them. God is the only Being in
the universe who needs nothing, or no one, to complete
Him. To venerate God means to give Him the recognition
He deserves, to acknowledge His superiority and to treat
Him with admiration and respect. This means that prayer is
much more than a way by which we can talk to God about
our problems and difficulties: it is a vehicle by which God
can increasingly reveal to us who and what He is.

This might surprise some Christians who think of prayer
merely as a means by which they can obtain things
from God. Prayer, first and foremost, is a communication
system through which God is able to reach deep into our
spirits, and impress upon us His superiority, His power
and His love. 'I will do whatever you ask in my name,'
said Jesus. And why? 'So that the Son may bring glory
to the Father' (John 14:13). If prayer does not begin by
giving God a pre-eminent place in our hearts and minds,
then it is not New Testament praying. The first petition in
the Lord's Prayer is not on our own behalf but on His!

Does this mean that we develop a mystical attitude
towards the term 'God'? No. In biblical times, names were
not just designations, but definitions. They had varied and
special meanings. A name stood for a person's character,
such as is demonstrated in 1 Samuel 18:30: 'David …
behaved himself more wisely than all Saul's servants, so
that his name was very dear and highly esteemed' (Amp).

The people did not esteem the letters of David's name. The statement means that David himself was esteemed. In Exodus 34:5–7 we read, 'Then the Lord ... announced the meaning of his name. "I am Jehovah, the merciful and gracious God," he said, "slow to anger and rich in steadfast love and truth"' (TLB). Here we are given not just the name of God but some of the characteristics that go under that name. He is merciful, gracious, long-suffering, and so on. In other words, the name of God is the composite of all His attributes. When we honour God's name, we honour Him. When, as God's children, we come to Him to honour His name, we do more than enter into a religious routine – we contemplate all that His name stands for, and reverence Him for what He is.

The phrase 'hallowed be your name' implies that prayer is first and foremost a recognition of God's character and a willingness to submit to it. Jesus put first the determining thing in prayer – God's character. If our petitions are not in line with His character, then, however eloquently or persistently we plead our cause, the answer will be a firm and categorical, 'No'. We are saying, in effect, 'Your character be revered first, before my desires or my petitions.' Any other kind of praying is contrary to Jesus' pattern.

Discussion Starters

1. How can we hallow something?

_____
_____
_____
_____

2. Why should we hallow God's name?

_____
_____
_____
_____

3. Which characteristics of God can you identify?

_____
_____
_____
_____

4. In which ways can we bring glory to God's name?

_____
_____
_____
_____

5. How did the psalmist hallow God?

_____
_____
_____
_____

6. How can we strike a balance between friendship with God and being in awe of His holiness?

_____

_____

_____

_____

7. How did Jesus hallow God's name?

_____

_____

_____

_____

8. Do you think that modern believers are 'too-matey' with the 'All-Mighty'?

_____

_____

_____

_____

Personal Application

One of the things that saddens me about the contemporary Christian Church is the way that some believers refer to the Almighty in terms that drag Him down to a kind of 'good buddy' relationship. They refer to the great God of creation as 'The Man Upstairs' or 'My Partner in the Sky'. When people talk about God in such low-level terms, they do Him an injustice. And it's not so much the terms but the image of God that lies behind those terms which is the real problem. He is the 'All-Mighty' not the 'All-Matey'. We must, of course, strike a balanced note on this issue, as Paul teaches that the Holy Spirit in our hearts prompts us to call God, not merely Father, but 'Daddy' (Rom. 8:15). Too much of the 'Daddy', however, can lead us, if we are not careful, into sloppy sentimentalism. I believe this is why, after the phrase 'Our Father', Jesus introduces us to another aspect of God – hallowed, holy, reverenced be His name. It is right that we think of God in familiar terms such as 'Daddy', but it is also right we remember that our heavenly Father is a God of majestic holiness and unsullied purity.

Seeing Jesus in the Scriptures

In one of His prayers, Jesus used the term, 'Holy Father' (John 17:11). Although He knew He was God's Son and had the most intimate relationship with God, Jesus was continually aware of God's holiness and sought to give Him the glory that was due to Him (John 12:28; 17:4).

WEEK 3

God's Kingdom Come

Opening Icebreaker

How many kings and queens of England can you name?

Bible Readings

- Daniel 4:28–37
- Matthew 6:19–34
- Luke 11:1–4
- Romans 14:17
- Colossians 1:9–23
- Revelation 11:15

Opening Our Eyes

Jesus, after making clear that the first consideration in prayer is to focus on God's character, puts as the next issue the establishing of God's kingdom. Just as the mariner has to get his bearings from the stars to be able to put into the right earthly port, so we have to get our eternal values straight before we begin to concentrate on temporal things.

What exactly does Jesus mean when He uses the word 'kingdom'? The word 'kingdom', *basileia* in the Greek, means 'rule' or 'reign'. The kingdom of God, then, is the rule or reign of God; His sovereignty, for which we are to pray. Jesus spoke of the kingdom as being in the present as well as in the future. In Luke 17:21 he said, 'the kingdom of God is within you'. Wherever there is a heart that is surrendered to the claims and demands of Jesus Christ, there the kingdom exists. Remember Jesus said, 'My kingdom is not of this world ...' (John 18:36). But there is a day coming, says Jesus in Matthew 8:11, when both small and great will sit side by side in the kingdom, and realise that in God's order of things there are no favourites. The Scripture tells us also that God has a kingdom that is established in the heavens (Heb. 12:22–28), and the phrase we are studying, 'Your kingdom come' – is a petition for God to let that kingdom extend to every area of the universe where His rule is resisted. We are thus introduced to another great purpose of prayer – transporting to all parts of the universe, across the bridge of prayer, the power that overcomes all sin, all rebellion and all evil.

One of the sad things about Church history is the fact that the Church has never really been gripped by the vision of the kingdom of God. It has taught about it, of course, but it has never put the kingdom where Jesus put it in His prayer, and given it the first consideration and the first allegiance. There are notable exceptions to what I am saying, of course, but by and large the Church has missed its way in this matter. No wonder the Church has stumbled from problem to problem when its priorities are lost or only marginally held. One theologian points out that when the Church drew up its creeds – the Apostles', the Athanasian, the Nicene – it mentioned the kingdom but once in all three of them, and then only marginally. The Church will never move into the dimension God has planned for it until it puts the kingdom where Jesus put it in this prayer – in a place of primary consideration and primary allegiance. Man-made empires come and go. Egypt came and went. Syria came and went. Babylon came and went. Greece came and went. Historians tell us that at least twenty-one former great civilisations are extinct. Earthly kingdoms go the way of all flesh – the debasing power of sin, decay, distress and destruction is inevitable. The kingdom of God, unlike earthly kingdoms, is destined for eternity and you and I are a part of it if we accept Jesus as our King. Note that Christ and the disciples were *in* the world but not *of* the world (John 15:19; 17:13–18). Oh that we would become so preoccupied with the kingdom of God that it would affect every part of our being, our thinking, our working and our praying.

Discussion Starters

1. What is the nature of God's kingdom?

_____

_____

_____

_____

2. In what sense is God's kingdom already here?

_____

_____

_____

_____

3. In what sense is God's kingdom still to come?

_____

_____

_____

_____

4. In what sense are we part of Satan's kingdom?

_____

_____

_____

_____

5. What is our role in God's kingdom?

_____

_____

_____

_____

6. How does a theocracy differ from a democracy?

_____

_____

_____

_____

7. Is democracy always a good thing? (You might like
to consider Numbers 13:26–14:12.)

_____

_____

_____

_____

8. Contrast Nebuchadnezzar's kingdom with God's
kingdom.

_____

_____

_____

_____

9. What does it mean to be in the world but not of
the world?

_____

_____

_____

_____

Personal Application

Any pattern of praying that does not make the kingdom a priority is not Christian praying. If you seek something else first then your life will be off-balance. A newspaper report on my desk tells of a small town in Alaska where all the electric clocks were showing the wrong time. The fault, it appears, was in the local power plant. It failed to run with systematic regularity, and thus all the electric clocks were 'out'. When your loyalty and primary concern is for something other than the kingdom of God, then everything in your life will be 'out', too.

Our own causes are valid only as they accord with the eternal cause of God. When I pray, 'Your kingdom come,' I am really praying, 'Lord, I pray that You will do whatever advances Your kingdom, whatever brings in Your rule and Your reign.' And, we might add – 'even though my own "cause" might have to be pushed aside.' What a prayer! What a challenge! No wonder the ancient Jewish Talmud said that 'the prayer in which there is no mention of the kingdom of God is no prayer at all'. It's only when we get the kingdom values straight that we can pray this prayer with assurance.

Seeing Jesus in the Scriptures

The kingdom of God was the motif running through everything Jesus did, for He made it the central note of His preaching and also His praying. He said, 'I must preach the good news of the kingdom of God to the other towns also, because that is why I was sent' (Luke 4:43).

WEEK 4

God's Will be Done

Opening Icebreaker

Choose one or more of the names of God from Week 2's Leader's Notes for a time of reflection, prayer and worship.

Bible Readings

- Psalm 40:6–8
- John 6:38–40
- Acts 9:10–19
- Romans 12:1–2
- Philippians 2:1–11
- Hebrews 10:5–22

Opening Our Eyes

We come today to the fifth clause in Jesus' pattern of praying: 'Your will be done on earth as it is in heaven'. It becomes obvious right away that if we are to know how God's will is to be done on earth, then we need to know how it is done in heaven. We ask ourselves therefore: how is the will of the Almighty followed by the angels in heaven?

First, it is followed unquestioningly. There is no discussion or debate amongst the angels over any of the Creator's directives. Here on earth the Lord has to prod and poke in order to get His servants moving, but in heaven no such prodding is necessary. Second, it is done speedily. Once a command is received, then the angels move with the utmost speed to do His bidding. They eagerly wait for the next command so they can hurry to accomplish it. How slow and sluggish are we, His earthly servants, by comparison. Third, it is done completely. The angels carry out God's bidding down to the tiniest detail. There are no alternatives, no omissions, no modifications to the divine orders. The will of God is done in fullest detail. A little girl, seven years of age, asked me once, 'Does an angel have a will?' I said, 'I think so.' 'Then how many wills are there in heaven?' she asked. 'Oh,' I said, 'there must be millions.' 'Wrong,' she said. 'There is only one. There were two once, but one got kicked out. Now God's will has full control' (Psa. 103:20–22). I was amazed at such clarity of thought from a seven-year-old. May the day soon dawn when the will of God is done on earth as it is done in heaven – unquestioningly, speedily and completely.

To pray the words, 'Your will be done', sometimes creates a conflict in us, particularly at such times when we know that God's will is the opposite of what we ourselves want. We, then, must consider whose will is to have precedence

God's Will be Done

WEEK | **FOUR**

– ours or God's. There are some Christians who pray,
'Your will be done', but they do it with a wrong attitude –
an attitude of rebellion and resentment. They believe that
they cannot escape the inevitable, and they become angry
about it. When they say the words, 'Your will be done',
they are almost said through clenched teeth. Other people
say the words, not necessarily out of resentment, but with
an attitude of passive resignation. They say the words,
'Your will be done', but what they mean is something
like this: 'Lord, I'm not very happy about the way things
are turning out, but I suppose You know best. So I'll go
along with it, and try my best to believe it's for the best.'

The proper attitude to the will of God, and the goal for
which we should aim, is one of rejoicing. It's not easy
to arrive at such an attitude, I know, but nevertheless
we must have it before us as the desired end. David, as
we saw in the passage before us today, prayed that way,
and so, on occasions, did others in the Scriptures. If we
can cultivate that attitude as the normal and characteristic
reaction to everything that happens around us – sorrow,
disappointment, disillusionment, frustration, disaster, loss,
bereavement – then such a spirit is more than a match for
anything. As someone has said, 'The Hallelujah of triumph
is louder than the Amen of resignation.' It is!

Discussion Starters

1. Is it correct to describe heaven as a totalitarian community?

2. Should we discuss God's will with Him?

3. When is it natural to do God's will?

4. When is it unnatural to do God's will?

5. What decisions did Jesus face in doing God's will?

6. How can we know what God's will is?

_____

_____

_____

_____

7. Why can we be confident that God's will is in our own best interests?

_____

_____

_____

_____

8. How can we, like Jesus, align our wills to God's will?

_____

_____

_____

_____

Personal Application

Most commentators believe the phrase 'on earth' has reference to the world of human beings here on this earth. One day this earth will be peopled with those who will do the will of God, not with resentment or resignation, but with rejoicing.

It's hard sometimes to pray, 'Your will be done', when we know that if God has His way, we will not get our way. Has that ever happened to you? The basic reason for this conflict is due to the major problem of the human heart – self-centredness. Paul, when describing a self-centred life and its results in Romans 6:21, ends by asking this question: 'Well, what did you gain then by it all? Nothing but what you are now ashamed of!' (Moffatt). The end was zero. That is the inevitable end of a self-centred life – nothing. The major thing that stands in the way of God performing His will in our lives utterly and completely is just that – self-centredness. Did Jesus know that when His disciples prayed this prayer, 'Your will be done', it would sometimes produce a conflict within them? I am sure He did. He nevertheless framed the statement because He knew that if we are to become effective in prayer, then we must face up to the question: whose will comes first – mine or God's? I must be willing to say, 'God, do what You want.' We should always remember that ultimately God's will is based on love, reconciliation and salvation (2 Pet. 3:9).

Seeing Jesus in the Scriptures

'... not my will, but yours be done' (Luke 22:42).

WEEK 5

Our Daily Needs

Opening Icebreaker

What are your favourite foods? What are the basic necessities of life today?

Bible Readings

- Genesis 1:29–31
- Numbers 11:4–9
- 1 Chronicles 29:10–16
- Psalm 104:10–28
- 2 Corinthians 9:6–15
- Philippians 4:4–13

Opening Our Eyes

The Lord's Prayer falls naturally into two divisions: the first division focusing upon God, and the second division focusing on ourselves. We come now to the second part of the prayer, the part which has to do with our physical, psychological and spiritual needs. This natural division once again reinforces the truth we have been seeing, that it is only when God is given His rightful place that we can have the proper perspective towards ourselves.

Jesus begins this part of the prayer by encouraging us to petition God for our physical needs: 'Give us this day our daily bread.' Some Christians believe that it is inappropriate for most of us who live in the Western hemisphere to give expression to these words as, they say, our problem is not so much where do we get the next meal, but how do we keep from eating the next meal! In an overfed, overweight society, so they say, our prayer ought to be: 'Lord, teach us self-discipline, and prevent us from eating more than we need.' At first glance, the phrase which Jesus used – 'Give us this day our daily bread' – does seem somewhat inappropriate, at least for most of us who live in Europe or North America. This prayer might be better uttered by some of the inhabitants of Asia or Africa. However, to take that view is to misunderstand the deep truth which Jesus wants us to absorb. He invites us to pray, 'Give us this day our daily bread', because when we say these words with sincerity and meaning, we build for ourselves a barrier against ingratitude. All that comes from God must be taken, not for granted, but with gratitude.

Of course some people argue that because Jesus said, '… your Father knows what you need before you ask him' (Matt. 6:8), then it is pointless to inform God of our physical needs. He knows them already – so they say. Here we touch the central value of prayer. Prayer is not

something by which we inform God of our needs, and
thus influence Him to give things to us. Prayer is designed
to influence us – it is we who are in need of this kind
of prayer, not God. Of course God knows what we are
in need of, but He also knows that unless we come face
to face daily with the fact that we are creatures of need,
then we can soon develop a spirit of independence, and
withdraw ourselves from close contact and fellowship
with Him. Prayer, then, is something we need. God may
not need to be told, but we need to tell Him. That's the
point. And unless we grasp it we can miss the primary
purpose of prayer. If we neglect to pray for our needs,
we will begin to take the blessings of life for granted and,
gradually, without at first realising it, we will succumb
to the senseless notion that we can provide for the
necessities of life, and that we are perfectly capable of
managing our own affairs, without any help from God.
When we think that way, it is not long before pride steps
in, and a kind of spiritual blindness settles upon us – a
blindness which blocks our vision in relation to God,
ourselves and others. The only way, therefore, that we
can build a barricade against this awful blight is to pray
daily for our needs and thank God for providing them.

Discussion Starters

1. What is the primary purpose of prayer?

2. Why should we pray about our daily needs?

3. How does ingratitude arise and why is it so damaging?

4. Is an attitude of gratitude a necessity for finding fulfilment in daily living?

5. How did the Israelites despise God?

6. How can we honour God for providing our daily needs?

7. What secret had Paul discovered for happiness?

8. How can we enjoy the good things in life without becoming materialistic? (See Luke 12:13–21; 1 Tim. 6:6–19.)

Personal Application

Paul says that God has created all food '… to be received with thanksgiving by those who believe and who know the truth' (1 Tim. 4:3). Can you see what this verse is saying? God has provided an incredible abundance of food that we might express our thanks to Him. The rest of the world indulges with little gratitude. Let's make sure that not one day passes without this prayer meaningfully crossing our lips: 'Give us this day our daily bread.' This is not a matter of merely saying grace before meals but of an inner attitude of gratitude for God's provision in our lives. We should also think wider than just food and also thank God and pray for our friends, finances, churches, homes and worldly goods that bring benefit into our lives. You could also consider how you could be a channel of God's provision for those who are less fortunate, either at home or overseas. 'The world of the generous gets larger and larger; the world of the stingy gets smaller and smaller' (Prov. 11:24, Message).

Seeing Jesus in the Scriptures

Although Jesus relegated our physical needs in favour of first seeking the kingdom, He nevertheless supernaturally fed thousands who were hungry (Matt. 14:13–21; 15:29–38), gave detailed instructions about a special meal (Mark 14:12–16), gave thanks for ordinary food (Luke 24:30) and prepared breakfast for the hungry disciples (John 21:9–13). He said that when we minister practically to those in need, we minister to Him (Matt. 25:31–46). Jesus was therefore not aloof from the daily issues of life and thanked God for His provision in meeting them.

WEEK 6

The Freedom of Forgiveness

Opening Icebreaker

What should a husband do if he has forgotten his wedding anniversary?

Bible Readings

- Psalm 32:1–7
- Psalm 51:1–17
- Matthew 6:14–15
- Matthew 18:21–22
- Luke 18:9–14
- Ephesians 4:25–32

Opening Our Eyes

What is the biggest single problem which faces us in human life? Some would say ill-health; others, lack of money; still others, uncertainty about the future, or fear of dying. My own view is that the biggest single problem with which human beings have to grapple, is the problem of guilt. A sense of guilt is the most powerfully destructive force in the personality. In extreme cases it can even drive people to suicide (like Judas in Matthew 27:3–5). We cannot live with guilt, that is, truly live.

Someone said that the point at which psychology and religion meet is at the point of guilt. Both Christianity and the social sciences underline what the human heart knows so well – it cannot live comfortably with guilt. There are some secular psychiatrists who take the attitude that guilt, being dangerous to the personality, must be dealt with by persuading their clients that there is no basis for their guilt feelings, that conscience and the moral universe are man-made concepts, and must be eliminated. There is nothing, they say, to feel guilty about, so, as some put it: 'Let bygones be bygones and wave goodbye to guilt.' It must be acknowledged that some ideas regarding guilt have to be dealt with in that way, for some guilt is false, and needlessly torments many sincere people. However, I am not talking here about *false* guilt. *Real* guilt needs to be properly dealt with, else it will corrode the personality. There is also *theological* guilt, where whether we feel it or not, we have broken God's law.

You cannot get away with guilt, either by waving goodbye to it or by bottling it up within you. Even the young doctor in A.J. Cronin's book *The Citadel* found his hidden inner problems were eventually revealed. When politics defeated his proposed health measures in a Welsh mining town, he sold his standards for money. After his wife's tragic death, he found in her handbag snapshots of himself taken during his crusading days. It reminded him of the man he might have been. He knew his pain was deserved, and he shouted at himself in a drunken stupor, 'You thought you could get away with it. You thought you were getting away with it. But ... you weren't.' Lady Macbeth, in Shakespeare's play, said, 'What, will these hands ne'er be clean? Here's the smell of the blood still. All the perfumes of Arabia will not sweeten this little hand.' Only the blood of Jesus Christ can erase the stain of guilt upon the human heart. When we pray, 'Forgive us our sins', we are asking for the reality that God promises to everyone who asks of Him. And the only way we can fail to experience it is simply by failing to ask.

In this prayer of Jesus, however, we have an adequate answer: 'Forgive us our trespasses, as we forgive those who trespass against us' (v.12). I prefer the word 'trespass' in preference to the word 'debt', as in our modern society the word 'debt' has come to have a monetary significance, and, by reason of this, has become somewhat narrowed. The word 'trespass' has a wider significance and implies an offence done against another – an intrusion into someone's rights. If we have fully accepted the forgiveness of God, and we know that our sins have been forgiven, then the result is a pervading sense of peace. The human heart cannot be put off by subterfuge: it needs reconciliation, forgiveness and assurance.

Discussion Starters

1. What are trespasses?

2. What is guilt?

3. How does guilt arise in the personality and how do people cope with it?

4. How is guilt linked to the conscience and a personal value system?

5. What is the difference between false human guilt, real human guilt and theological guilt?

6. What is the difference between confession and repentance?

7. What does receiving God's forgiveness free us from?

8. Why should we forgive others?

9. What do we need to do in order for God to forgive us?

10. Why was only the tax collector justified? (See Luke 18:9–14.)

Personal Application

Jesus adds a condition to the request for forgiveness. He says that we can only ask God to forgive us our trespasses when we are willing to forgive those who have trespassed against us. Paul says in Ephesians 1:7, 'In him we have redemption through his blood, the forgiveness of our trespasses, according to the riches of his grace ...' (RSV). Grace – that's the basis of our forgiveness when we first come to Christ. But although we have received that forgiveness, we can never enjoy freedom from defilements in our Christian walk unless we are ready to extend the forgiveness God has given us to those who have hurt or offended us. This is an extremely important and serious issue, and one that we must not treat lightly, for if we fail to forgive those who have offended us, we break the bridge over which God's forgiveness flows into us.

Don't try to forget things, don't try to smooth them over and don't drive them into the subconscious. Get them up and out. A woman visited her doctor and asked him to give her a special ointment to smooth over her abscess. When the doctor refused and said it must be lanced, she left his surgery and went home. In a few days the poison had spread through her system and killed her. Unbelievable? I actually knew this lady. I beg you, when facing the issue which is confronting us this week, don't ask for a Band-aid or a halfway measure. Get it out. Forgive.

 Seeing Jesus in the Scriptures

'Father forgive them ...' (Luke 23:34).

WEEK 7

Overcoming Evil and Seeing God's Glory

Opening Icebreaker

What has impacted you most from our previous studies?

Bible Readings

- Matthew 4:1–11
- Matthew 16:21–23; 26:36–46
- Luke 22:39–46
- James 1:1–15
- 1 Corinthians 10:12–13
- 1 Peter 5:7

Opening Our Eyes

An immediate problem presents itself in this section, and it is one which theologians have debated for centuries. If temptation is necessary to our growth (as we grapple – we grow), are we really expected to pray that God will not do what He must do in order to accomplish His work within us? After all, Jesus was *led* by the Spirit into the wilderness to be tempted by the devil (Luke 4:1) and James tells us to 'count it all joy when you fall into divers temptation' (James 1:2, AV).

The view which I personally regard as the clearest meaning of our Lord's words was originally given by Chrysostom, an Early Church Father. He said,

> This particular petition is the most natural appeal of human weakness as it faces danger. It's the cry of a heart that despises and abhors even the possibility of sin. It is the admission of human weakness, and a recognition of our human tendency to stumble on into folly.

Perhaps, in order to see these words in a clear light, we need to set them against our Lord's experience in the Garden of Gethsemane. He prayed, 'My Father, if it is possible, may this cup be taken from me' (Matt. 26:39). Jesus knew that the only way to accomplish redemption for the human race was by way of the cross. Nevertheless, because He was human as well as divine, He gave expression to His humanity, even though, as the writer to the Hebrews said, He endured the cross for the joy that was set before Him (Heb. 12:2). You see, although Jesus knew that the cross had to be experienced in all its horror and torment if men and women were to be redeemed, He still gave expression to His human feelings of dread and apprehension. Jesus did not feel guilty about this demonstration of His humanity, neither was God disappointed by His words. The expression of our human weakness is a necessary part of prayer.

Jesus' statement 'Lead us not into temptation' is not intended to be something that relates to the mind, but something that relates to the heart. It is as if Jesus is saying: 'Even though your mind understands that as you face temptation and overcome it you become stronger in God, there is still a part of you – your emotions – that feels it would rather not face the pressures. I understand this. I have been in that situation Myself. So I will provide a prayer framework for you that will enable you to express not so much your thoughts, but your feelings. It will be an admission of your feelings of weakness, but it will also be a release, for if your fears are not expressed, they will be repressed, and will go "underground" to cause trouble. So these words will provide you with what you need – an opportunity to give vent to your inner feelings of reluctance at facing temptation.' God recognises that I am not just an intellectual being but an emotional being, and builds into His pattern of prayer a safety valve that lets me express my inner feelings.

The prayer ends in some translations (for example the AV), as it begins, with an assertion of God's majesty and glory: 'For thine is the kingdom' – now. Despite appearances to the contrary, we are reminded that God has never abdicated His position as Ruler of the universe.

Discussion Starters

1. Why should we express our feelings to God?

_____
_____
_____

2. What temptations did Jesus face and how did He overcome them?

_____
_____
_____
_____

3. Why did Jesus pray to avoid the cross?

_____
_____
_____

4. How can temptation be both bad and good for us?

_____
_____
_____

5. Identify the thoughts and feelings of Jesus before and after His prayer in Gethsemane.

_____
_____
_____

6. How can we overcome temptation? (See Heb. 2:14–18; 4:14–16.)

_____

_____

_____

_____

7. Explain Jesus' statement, 'The spirit is willing, but the body is weak' (Matt 26:41).

_____

_____

_____

_____

8. How does God deliver us from evil?

_____

_____

_____

_____

9. How do you intend to apply the teaching of Jesus in the Lord's Prayer to your own prayer life?

_____

_____

_____

_____

Personal Application

The final ushering in of God's kingdom is yet to take place, but that does not mean that He is taking a back seat in the world's affairs. God wants to reign through us! We need not wait for the day when dramatically and spectacularly the great God of the universe demonstrates His imperial power. He sounds forth a rallying cry now. Respond to it, I urge you, with a fresh consecration of purpose, and dedicate yourself to letting Him reign through you today.

If we understand the Lord's Prayer correctly, there is really nothing more to be said when we come to this matter of prayer. This does not mean, of course, that prayer has to be limited to simply reciting these statements of Jesus, but it does mean that the issues He deals with cover the entire gamut of human need, and are the pattern for all adequate and effective praying. When we fail to cover the issues raised in Jesus' pattern of prayer, expanding on them in our own words, we deny ourselves the true power that lies in prayer. Follow the pattern and you find the power.

Seeing Jesus in the Scriptures

At Gethsemane we see Jesus under extreme pressure and temptation to reject God's will and evade all the physical, emotional and spiritual pain of crucifixion and separation from His Father. He is in agony and 'almost dying of sorrow' (Matt. 26:38, Amp). Yet after intense and emotional prayer He embraces God's will and positively faces His future, 'Rise, let us go! Here comes my betrayer!' (Matt. 26:46).

Leader's Notes

Week 1: Father in Heaven

Opening Icebreaker
The concept of God as our Father is fundamental to a fulfilling and effective prayer life. It is therefore vital that we ascribe to God all the good qualities of fatherhood irrespective of our own experiences. I suggest you begin each week by praying the Lord's Prayer together and then ask for His help to fully understand and implement the insights of that session.

Bible Readings
A number of additional references are given that would be useful to read. Also you could find specific examples of how Jesus related to people in ways that revealed God's Father heart.

Aim of the Session
We must focus upon God before we begin to focus on ourselves. How many times, when making an approach to God in prayer, have we gone immediately into a series of petitions that have to do with our problems, our difficulties and our circumstances? And so, by focusing our attention on what is troubling us, we end up wondering whether or not God is big enough, or strong enough, to help us.

In the first six words of the Lord's Prayer, Jesus shows us a better way. He tells us to take a slow, calm, reassuring gaze at God – at His tenderness, His eagerness to give, His weariless patience and untiring love. The result of this, of course, is that we develop a calmness and tranquillity in our spirit which means we will no longer find it necessary to plunge into a panicky flood of words.

God offers us infinite resources for the asking and the taking – Himself. The first moments of prayer should, therefore, be contemplative, reflective, meditative. As we gaze upon God and His infinite resources, we take, as someone put it, 'a time exposure to God'. His adequacy and sufficiency are printed indelibly upon us. No matter, then, what difficulties and problems face us – we are more than a match for them. The vision of His greatness puts the whole of life in its proper perspective. In the words of the poet Richard Chenevix Trench, 'We kneel, how weak – we rise, how full of power.'

Is God a Father to all men and women everywhere, or only to those who are committed members of the Christian Church? For many years now liberally-minded theologians have taught that God is everyone's Father, so we are all His children, and thus all brothers and sisters. This teaching, known as the universal brotherhood of man, makes conversion unnecessary, and puts to one side the redemptive sufferings of Christ on the cross.

The Bible teaches that God is a Father in two senses. Firstly, He is the Father of the human family by virtue of creation. Malachi 2:10 says, 'Have we not all one Father? Did not one God create us?' In Acts 17:29 Paul said, 'we are God's offspring'. In the sense of creation, yes, God is our Father. In the sense of a familial relationship, He is not. Jesus said in John 8:44 to the Jewish leaders, 'You belong to your father, the devil.' Quite clearly, the fatherhood of God is seen in the Bible in two senses. He is the Father of all men and women because He is their Creator, but He has another family – a family within a family – consisting of those who have committed themselves to Jesus Christ, the Son.

It is interesting to note that religious people were offended by Jesus using the word 'Father' to describe His relationship with God. They would never have addressed God in this way, thinking that the term Father implied a familiarity that was blasphemous and impossible for mere human beings (see John 5:18). Yet here was the greatest revelation of all.

Week 2: Honouring God's Name

Opening Icebreaker

Names were particularly important in biblical times because they carried special meanings and often revealed something about the person (eg in Genesis 32:28, Jacob (supplanter, cheat) became Israel (prince with God). God's name is to be honoured because of all it means.

Bible Readings

The readings focus on the Old Testament names and attributes of God, but as an extended study you might also research the names and 'I ams' of Christ (eg Isa. 9:6; John 6:35; 8:12).

Aim of the Session

The ancient Israelites attached such sacredness to the name of God that they would not say it aloud. They thought that hallowing God's name meant hallowing the name itself. How utterly foolish and absurd! They paid honour to the actual letters of God's name, yet, on occasions, thought nothing about disobeying His word and denying His truth. One great Hebrew scholar points out that there is no such word as Jehovah in the Hebrew language, although it appears in English translations of the Old Testament. The name of God in Exodus 3:14, where the Almighty gave His name to Moses, 'I AM WHO I AM', is Yahweh: the English equivalent of which is Jehovah. The Israelites would not say the word Yahweh, and eventually the vowels were taken out and mixed with the consonants of another Hebrew word to form the word

'Adonai'. This was done as a device to avoid having to say the real word 'Yahweh'. To hallow God's name is not to avoid its pronunciation but rather to awaken ourselves to the greatness, majesty and ability of the One to whom we pray.

The various names of God used in the Bible reveal something of His attributes. Here is a simplified list of some of them that you could use in a period of reflection and worship:

Elohim	*The Strong Faithful One*	Genesis 1:26
El-Shaddai	*God the Enough or Sufficient One*	Genesis 17:1
Jehovah Jireh	*The Lord will Provide*	Genesis 22:14
Jehovah Rapha	*The Lord who Heals*	Exodus 15:26
Jehovah Nissi	*The Lord Our Banner*	Exodus 17:15
Jehovah Shalom	*The Lord Our Peace*	Judges 6:24
Jehovah Ra-ah	*The Lord Our Shepherd*	Psalm 23:1
Jehovah Tsidkenu	*The Lord Our Righteousness*	Jeremiah 23:6
Jehovah M'kaddesh	*The Lord who Makes Holy*	Leviticus 20:8
Jehovah Shammah	*The Lord is There*	Ezekiel 48:35
Jesus	*Saviour*	Matthew 1:21
Immanuel	*God with Us*	Matthew 1:23

Father	*Loving Parent, Provider and Protector*	Luke 11:13

Week 3: God's Kingdom Come

Opening Icebreaker

A simple exercise to start us thinking about the concept of a kingdom. However, in the United Kingdom the monarch has limited powers because we live in a democracy in which the people rule. God's kingdom is a theocracy where He rules.

Bible Readings

The readings emphasise the priority, superiority and eternity of God's kingdom.

Aim of the Session

Philosophers have said that if we are to live effectively and securely in this world, we must have a world-view of things – a cosmic framework in which to live, think and work. The Germans call it *Weltanschauung* – the big picture. When we have such a big picture, it gives a sense of validity and meaning to all we do. It makes us feel we are part of a universal purpose. Many modern thinkers believe that the reason why there is so much insecurity in the hearts of men and women is because there is a breakdown of that world frame of reference. One writer says, 'Modern man is homesick. He is going on a hand-to-mouth existence day by day, and what he does and thinks does not seem to be related to the Whole. This has made life empty and jittery because it is insecure.' The Chinese have a saying, 'In a broken nest there are no whole eggs.' The nest – the world in which we live and think and work – has been broken up by sin and, therefore, our central unity has gone. This can be seen on a small scale when the home is broken. Many of the people in young offenders' institutions come from broken homes. Why? The framework in which they have lived has broken down and has left them inwardly disrupted and confused. As a consequence morals break down. Can you see now why Jesus taught us to have a world-view of things? With our eyes focused on the kingdom, we know that at the heart of things there is utter security.

We must not forget that there exists in the universe another kingdom – the kingdom of Satan. The Bible shows us that in the ages past there was just one kingdom, the kingdom of God, but, through the sin and rebellion of an angel named Lucifer (now known as Satan), another kingdom was established over which the Prince of Darkness rules and reigns. Every person born into the world since Adam (with the single exception of Jesus Christ), comes under the dominion of Satan, and is, in fact, classified as a citizen of the devil's kingdom. Satan is regarded as the prince of this world (John 12:31; 14:30; 16:11; Eph. 2:1–2) and the prince of demons (Matt. 12:24). When, through conversion, we become followers of the Lord Jesus Christ, our citizenship is immediately changed, and we become citizens of the kingdom of God (Col. 1:13). Once we receive this new citizenship, whether we realise it or not, we are thrust into the front line of the age-long conflict which has existed between God and Satan, and we become participators in the Almighty's plan to bring about Satan's defeat, and to bring the universe once again under the control of God and His kingdom. Standing as we do on the cutting edge between the kingdom of God and the kingdom of Satan, the Almighty has given us a weapon with which to fight, that is the most powerful in all the armouries of heaven. That weapon is prayer. Our citizenship in God's kingdom entitles and enables us to pray, 'Your kingdom come.' And when uttered with sincerity and trust, those words spell out, every time they are spoken, the ultimate triumph of the kingdom of God.

Week 4: God's Will be Done

Opening Icebreaker

It has been said that nothing has been taught until something has been learnt and nothing has been learnt until something has been applied and implemented. Knowledge is worthless unless it is used, and can even have a negative effect upon us (1 Cor. 8:1–3). The purpose of studying the Bible is to change our thinking and behaviour. The purpose of this study is to develop our understanding of prayer in order not that we might know more about prayer, but that we might pray more. This activity, then, is an opportunity to put some of our teaching into practice.

Bible Readings

When we have God's Word in our heart (Psa. 40:8) and the Holy Spirit influencing our thoughts (Rom. 8:5–14) our natural desire is to do God's will. Even when this causes us personal sacrifice, we freely choose God's will above our own desires because we trust our heavenly Father's love and wisdom more than our instincts for self-comfort and self-preservation. We may still, however, discuss God's will with Him, as did Ananias, Abraham (Gen. 18:16–33), Gideon (Judges 6) and Jesus.

Aim of the Session

Heaven can be described as a totalitarian society where God's will reigns supreme and unquestioned. We are rather afraid of the word 'totalitarian' here on earth as it brings to mind oppressive regimes where individualism is discouraged or repressed. I recognise that the word has negative connotations because of this, but, make no mistake about it, heaven is a totalitarian community. Those reading these lines who have had some experience of totalitarianism might say, 'What? Are we to emerge from one totalitarian system to become involved in another?' The answer is yes. And God's totalitarianism is more thorough-going and absolute than any totalitarian regime on earth. However, there is a profound difference. When you obey the will of God fully and completely, you find perfect freedom. When you obey other totalitarian systems, you find utter bondage, for they are not in line with the way you were designed to live. As the stomach and poison are incompatible, and when brought together produce disruption and death, so your being and 'other-than-the-will-of-God' ways are not made for each other, and produce disruption and death. However, as the stomach thrives on good wholesome food, and the two are made for each other, and bring health and life, so the will of God and your being are made for each other, and when brought together produce health, life and fulfilment.

There are many in this universe who think like Ephraim, of whom God complained, 'I wrote for them the many things of my law, but they regarded them as something alien' (Hosea 8:12). Ephraim felt that God's laws were foreign sayings – things that were unnatural and caused pain. But the will of God and the human will are not alien. They were made for each other. The expression is inadequate, but it is the best way I know of explaining the fact that my will functions best when it acts and behaves in accordance with His will. We must take hold of this until it becomes a basic axiom: my will and God's will are not alien. When I find His will, I find my own. I am fulfilled when I make Him my centre; I am frustrated when I make myself the centre. And if you are afraid that this depletes you as a person, or makes you into a robot or automaton by subduing your individuality, then your fear is quite groundless. You are really at your best only when you are doing the will of God. Then all parts of your personality are drawn to vitality and fulfilment.

Week 5: Our Daily Needs

Opening Icebreaker

We need to truly appreciate all that we have because to take things for granted is to devalue what God has provided and deny ourselves the pleasure of fully enjoying so much of our daily lives. We should not wait for a catastrophe of war or natural disaster to be thankful for what we have.

Bible Readings

Look out for attitudes of gratitude and acts of appreciation.

Aim of the Session

I find it greatly encouraging that the God of creation, who is infinitely holy, and who holds the universe in His hand, cares that my physical needs are met. This implies that God regards our bodies as important. He designed them and engineered them, and is interested in the way they function. Some Christians regard it as 'unspiritual' to pray about the needs of the body, but, as Jesus pointed out, this is really where our personal petitions ought to begin. While Jesus endeavoured to get His hearers to keep their values straight, by saying that the spiritual was all important – 'But seek first his [God's] kingdom ...' (Matt. 6:33) – He nevertheless put the body in its rightful place, as being a matter of great concern. The Father, we are told, guarantees our physical needs if we seek first the kingdom of God. Most of the promises in the Bible have to do with spiritual truth, but never to the exclusion of the physical. How much spiritual use would we be to our heavenly Father if He didn't meet our basic physical needs?

The term bread is regarded by most Bible teachers as a broad term for food. Just think for a moment what God has provided in the way of nourishment for His children. He has provided food in the grains of wheat, barley and so on, and, according to Genesis 43:11 and Numbers 11:5,

He has provided nuts, vegetables, melons and a whole host of other things. Keep looking in God's pantry and you will find food plants such as grapes, raisins, olives and apples. In addition to this, there are animals which provide food, such as oxen, sheep and goats, as well as different kinds of fowl. Then there are fish, and according to Leviticus chapter 11, even four types of insects! How thrilling is His bountiful provision. You and I eat nothing that did not come from the earth, and every element in it is the work of the creative hand of God. Not to recognise that is indeed the height of ingratitude.

There are many difficulties and problems facing us today in relation to economy, but the issue is not really that the earth cannot provide enough food. If there is a failure, it is a failure of distribution, not a failure in production. The food is there, but it is not properly apportioned. The one-time Prime Minister of India, Mrs Gandhi, said that there are enough resources in India to feed that nation entirely, and then export two-thirds of what it produces. How wrong it is to blame God for the fact that thousands of people die of starvation each year. The fault is not in Him, but in us.

In this section we are really talking about God's provision. Although we have focused on food, there is also the matter of water, shelter, warmth, clothing, friendships, religious freedom, work, fuel and so on. Recent flooding in England has shown how fragile life can be without even water to drink or use for washing. Drought and disease in cattle and poultry has dramatically affected food production in recent years and shown the folly of simply 'taking things for granted'.

Week 6: The Freedom of Forgiveness

Opening Icebreaker

Whatever offence has been committed, there are generally several common steps that lead to absolution. These would include apology, penance and request for forgiveness. For example, 'I'm sorry', a box of chocolates and meal in a restaurant and an appeal to 'kiss and make up'! The 'penance' is not so much a bribe or a fine but a genuine attempt at reparation for the pain caused and evidences desire for reconciliation.

Bible Readings

Notice particularly in the Psalms the corrosive acid of guilt on the personality and the joy of salvation when sins are forgiven. Proverbs 30:12 speaks of proud and godless people who consider themselves faultless like the Pharisee in Luke 18:11. But where there is no acknowledgement of wrong there can be no forgiveness (1 John 1:9).

Aim of the Session

This second section of Jesus' pattern of prayer takes in every level of human life: the physical, the psychological and the spiritual. 'Give us this day' refers to the physical part of life. 'Forgive us our trespasses' has to do with the psychological part of life (the emotions, the thoughts and the will), and 'Lead us not into temptation' has to do with the spiritual part of life. The subject of forgiveness is part of a major Christian doctrine of the atonement, which would really require a separate study guide. However, we can in this session explore some of the important principles involved to experience the freedom of forgiveness in our own lives. We can be free from the feelings of guilt, we can be free from the voices of accusation and condemnation and we can be free from the effects of sin that would damage our fellowship with God. Sin separates us from those we have sinned against (Isa. 59:2). Where we were once separated from God and others we can be reconciled or 'at-one' with them.

Feelings of guilt are inevitably related to the functioning of the conscience which itself is greatly influenced by the prevailing moral climate of the society in which we live. For example, homosexual acts were once regarded as 'wrong', but society now deems them part of an acceptable alternative lifestyle. Owning slaves was regarded as 'right' but is now regarded as 'wrong'. A Bible study on 'conscience' reveals a fascinating explanation of human motivation and activity. What may be acceptable to me may be offensive to someone else (1 Cor. 8:4–13). It is because some have a corrupted or dysfunctional conscience (1 Tim. 4:1–5; Titus 1:15) that they regard pure activities as sinful and sinful activities as pure. So they will feel guilty when they should not, and will not feel guilty when they should. That is why we should not solely operate on the principle, 'let your conscience be your guide'. Instead, beyond personal and societal standards, there are the absolute standards of a holy God. To break His standards is to incur theological guilt, which is irrespective of our own feelings. Thus John writes, 'If we claim to be without sin, we deceive ourselves and the truth is not in us (1 John 1:8). Psalm 66:18 says, 'If I had not confessed the sin in my heart, the Lord would not have listened' (NLT). Although our dysfunctional conscience may not prevent us from indulging in sinful activity, God can awaken it to convict and restore us (eg 'conscience-stricken' [John 8:9, Amp], 'he will convict the world of guilt' [John 16:8] and 'pricks' of conscience [Acts 9:5, AV]).

The issue of forgiving others is a crucial element in the Lord's Prayer and a subject Jesus visited more than once (Matt. 5:23–24; 18:21–35). Holding on to grudges is sinful.

Week 7: Overcoming Evil and Seeing God's Glory

Opening Icebreaker
Reiteration and personal expression are important principles in the learning process and so particularly important in our last session together.

Bible Readings
The alternative Gethsemane accounts highlight different aspects of our understanding of temptation and how it may be overcome. For example, Jesus was in anguish in prayer *after* an angel strengthened Him, whereas we might think that an angel would deliver us from anguish. Notice also that this was not a quick routine prayer for deliverance but a powerful struggle and outpouring of emotions reminiscent of some of the Psalms (eg Psalm 42). Although our spirit is willing to do God's will, our natural human desires are so powerful that we need to watch and pray otherwise we are in danger of falling into temptation. Even Jesus did not presume His own unrivalled spiritual strength was sufficient by itself to overcome temptation, but prevailed fasting in the desert through knowing and quoting God's Word, and then in Gethsemane through intense prayer. We do well to remember the example of other strong believers such as John Mark and Demas who were fellow workers with Paul (Acts 13:5; Col. 4:14; Philem. 1:24). However, both deserted Paul, particularly Demas, who was tempted by the love of the world (Acts 15:37–38; 2 Tim. 4:10). We do indeed need to 'be careful that [we] don't fall!' (1 Cor. 10:12). Even Peter, who was adamant that he would rather die than desert Jesus, eventually disowned Him (Matt. 26:31–35,69–75). Our humble and earnest prayer not to be led into temptation and be delivered from evil is therefore an absolutely essential part of our petitions to God.

Aim of the Session

Rationally, I may perceive that temptation does a perfecting work in my personality, yet in my feelings, if I am honest, I would prefer not to face it. Our emotions, as well as our intellect, are taken into consideration by our Lord when laying down for us this pattern of prayer. He knows that to deny our feelings is to work against the personality and not with it. Psychologists tell us that the denial of feelings is the first step towards a nervous breakdown. Negative feelings must be handled carefully, for if repressed they are like the Chinese pirates of the past who used to hide in the hold of a vessel and then rise up when the ship was out on the open sea in order to attempt to capture and possess it.

One of the most fascinating and helpful insights I have ever found in my study of human personality is the fact that we don't have to act on our negative feelings, but we do have to acknowledge them. If we say with our minds: 'Come on, temptation, I'm ready for you', and deny the fact that our emotions feel differently, then this pretence, that the feelings are not there, invites trouble into the personality. When, however, we acknowledge the feelings, and admit they are there, we rob them of their power to hurt us. I see this psychological mechanism wonderfully catered for in the words of Jesus which we are considering. They are the framework in which our feelings can have a vote also. Thus, though not acted upon, they are not denied.

The aim of this entire study guide has been to emphasise that the Lord's Prayer is not primarily a series of words to be recited but a model to be followed. In this model we can use our own words to develop our relationship with our Father, we seek His purposes first before our own needs, we truly confess sin, we forgive others and we seek God's help to live righteous lives in His eternal kingdom. For ever. Amen!

National Distributors

UK: (and countries not listed below)

CWR, Waverley Abbey House, Waverley Lane, Farnham, Surrey GU9 8EP.
Tel: (01252) 784700 Outside UK (44) 1252 784700 Email: mail@cwr.org.uk

AUSTRALIA: KI Entertainment, Unit 21 317-321 Woodpark Road, Smithfield, New South Wales
2164. Tel: 1 800 850 777 Fax: 02 9604 3699 Email: sales@kientertainment.com.au

CANADA: David C Cook Distribution Canada, PO Box 98, 55 Woodslee Avenue, Paris, Ontario N3L
3E5. Tel: 1800 263 2664 Email: sandi.swanson@davidccook.ca

GHANA: Challenge Enterprises of Ghana, PO Box 5723, Accra.
Tel: (021) 222437/223249 Fax: (021) 226227 Email: ceg@africaonline.com.gh

HONG KONG: Cross Communications Ltd, 1/F, 562A Nathan Road, Kowloon.
Tel: 2780 1188 Fax: 2770 6229 Email: cross@crosshk.com

INDIA: Crystal Communications, 10-3-18/4/1, East Marredpalli, Secunderabad – 500026, Andhra
Pradesh. Tel/Fax: (040) 27737145 Email: crystal_edwj@rediffmail.com

KENYA: Keswick Books and Gifts Ltd, PO Box 10242-00400, Nairobi. Tel: (020) 2226047/312639
Email: sales.keswick@africaonline.co.ke

MALAYSIA: Canaanland Distributors Sdn Bhd, No. 25 Jalan PJU 1A/41B, NZX Commercial Centre,
Ara Jaya, 47301 Petaling Jaya, Selangor. Tel: (03) 7885 0540/1/2 Fax: (03) 7885 0545
Email: info@canaanland.com.my

Salvation Publishing & Distribution Sdn Bhd, 23 Jalan SS 2/64, 47300 Petaling Jaya, Selangor.
Tel: (03) 78766411/78766797 Fax: (03) 78757066/78756360 Email: info@salvationbookcentre.com

NEW ZEALAND: KI Entertainment, Unit 21 317-321 Woodpark Road, Smithfield, New South Wales
2164, Australia. Tel: 0 800 850 777 Fax: +612 9604 3699 Email: sales@kientertainment.com.au

NIGERIA: FBFM, Helen Baugh House, 96 St Finbarr's College Road, Akoka, Lagos.
Tel: (01) 7747429/4700218/825775/827264 Email: fbfm_1@yahoo.com

PHILIPPINES: OMF Literature Inc, 776 Boni Avenue, Mandaluyong City. Tel: (02) 531 2183
Fax: (02) 531 1960 Email: gloadlaon@omflit.com

SINGAPORE: Alby Commercial Enterprises Pte Ltd, 95 Kallang Avenue #04-00, AIS Industrial
Building, 339420. Tel: (65) 629 27238 Fax: (65) 629 27235 Email: marketing@alby.com.sg

SRI LANKA: Christombu Publications (Pvt) Ltd, Bartleet House, 65 Braybrooke Place, Colombo 2.
Tel: (9411) 2421073/2447665 Email: christombupublications@gmail.com

USA: David C Cook Distribution Canada, PO Box 98, 55 Woodslee Avenue, Paris, Ontario N3L 3E5,
Canada. Tel: 1800 263 2664 Email: sandi.swanson@davidccook.ca

CWR is a Registered Charity - Number 294387
CWR is a Limited Company registered in England - Registration Number 1990308

Courses and seminars

Publishing and media

Conference facilities

Transforming lives

CWR's vision is to enable people to experience personal transformation through applying God's Word to their lives and relationships.

Our Bible-based training and resources help people around the world to:
• Grow in their walk with God
• Understand and apply Scripture to their lives
• Resource themselves and their church
• Develop pastoral care and counselling skills
• Train for leadership
• Strengthen relationships, marriage and family life and much more.

Our insightful writers provide daily Bible-reading notes and other resources for all ages, and our experienced tutors and presenters have gained an international reputation for excellence and effectiveness.

CWR's Training and Conference Centres in Surrey and East Sussex, England, provide excellent facilities in idyllic settings – ideal for both learning and spiritual refreshment.

CWR Applying God's Word
to everyday life and relationships

CWR, Waverley Abbey House,
Waverley Lane, Farnham,
Surrey GU9 8EP, UK

Telephone: **+44 (0)1252 784700**
Email: **info@cwr.org.uk**
Website: **www.cwr.org.uk**

Registered Charity No 294387
Company Registration No 1990308

Dramatic new resources

Bible Genres – Hearing what the Bible really says
by Andy Peck

Explore seven of the major genres used by writers of the Bible and consider how each style reflects more deeply what God is saying in His Word.

ISBN: 978-1-85345-987-0

Daniel – Living boldly for God
by Christine Platt

Discover how Daniel lived boldly for God in a hostile culture and consider his extreme courage in a crisis. Reflect on how we can apply what we learn as we seek to live boldly for God in our own lives.

ISBN: 978-1-85345-986-3

Also available in the bestselling
Cover to Cover Bible Study Series

1 Corinthians
Growing a Spirit-filled church
ISBN: 978-1-85345-374-8

2 Corinthians
Restoring harmony
ISBN: 978-1-85345-551-3

1 Timothy
Healthy churches –
effective Christians
ISBN: 978-1-85345-291-8

23rd Psalm
The Lord is my shepherd
ISBN: 978-1-85345-449-3

2 Timothy and Titus
Vital Christianity
ISBN: 978-1-85345-338-0

Acts 1–12
Church on the move
ISBN: 978-1-85345-574-2

Acts 13–28
To the ends of the earth
ISBN: 978-1-85345-592-6

Barnabas
Son of encouragement
ISBN: 978-1-85345-911-5

Bible Genres
Hearing what the Bible really says
ISBN: 978-1-85345-987-0

Daniel
Living boldly for God
ISBN: 978-1-85345-986-3

Ecclesiastes
Hard questions and
spiritual answers
ISBN: 978-1-85345-371-7

Elijah
A man and his God
ISBN: 978-1-85345-575-9

Ephesians
Claiming your inheritance
ISBN: 978-1-85345-229-1

Esther
For such a time as this
ISBN: 978-1-85345-511-7

Fruit of the Spirit
Growing more like Jesus
ISBN: 978-1-85345-375-5

Galatians
Freedom in Christ
ISBN: 978-1-85345-648-0

Genesis 1–11
Foundations of reality
ISBN: 978-1-85345-404-2

God's Rescue Plan
Finding God's fingerprints
on human history
ISBN: 978-1-85345-294-9

Great Prayers of the Bible
Applying them to our lives today
ISBN: 978-1-85345-253-6

Hebrews
Jesus – simply the best
ISBN: 978-1-85345-337-3

Hosea
The love that never fails
ISBN: 978-1-85345-290-1

Isaiah 1-39
Prophet to the nations
ISBN: 978-1-85345-510-0

Isaiah 40-66
Prophet of restoration
ISBN: 978-1-85345-550-6

James
Faith in action
ISBN: 978-1-85345-293-2

Jeremiah
The passionate prophet
ISBN: 978-1-85345-372-4

John's Gospel
Exploring the seven miraculous signs
ISBN: 978-1-85345-295-6

Joseph
The power of forgiveness and reconciliation
ISBN: 978-1-85345-252-9

Judges 1-8
The spiral of faith
ISBN: 978-1-85345-681-7

Judges 9-21
Learning to live God's way
ISBN: 978-1-85345-910-8

Mark
Life as it is meant to be lived
ISBN: 978-1-85345-233-8

Moses
Face to face with God
ISBN: 978-1-85345-336-6

Names of God
Exploring the depths of God's character
ISBN: 978-1-85345-680-0

Nehemiah
Principles for life
ISBN: 978-1-85345-335-9

Parables
Communicating God on earth
ISBN: 978-1-85345-340-3

Philemon
From slavery to freedom
ISBN: 978-1-85345-453-0

Philippians
Living for the sake of the gospel
ISBN: 978-1-85345-421-9

Prayers of Jesus
Hearing His heartbeat
ISBN: 978-1-85345-647-3

Proverbs
Living a life of wisdom
ISBN: 978-1-85345-373-1

Revelation 1-3
Christ's call to the Church
ISBN: 978-1-85345-461-5

Revelation 4-22
The Lamb wins! Christ's final victory
ISBN: 978-1-85345-411-0

Rivers of Justice
Responding to God's call to righteousness today
ISBN: 978-1-85345-339-7

Ruth
Loving kindness in action
ISBN: 978-1-85345-231-4

The Covenants
God's promises and their relevance today
ISBN: 978-1-85345-255-0

The Divine Blueprint
God's extraordinary power in ordinary lives
ISBN: 978-1-85345-292-5

The Holy Spirit
Understanding and experiencing Him
ISBN: 978-1-85345-254-3

The Image of God
His attributes and character
ISBN: 978-1-85345-228-4

The Kingdom
Studies from Matthew's Gospel
ISBN: 978-1-85345-251-2

The Letter to the Colossians
In Christ alone
ISBN: 978-1-85345-405-9

The Letter to the Romans
Good news for everyone
ISBN: 978-1-85345-250-5

The Lord's Prayer
Praying Jesus' way
ISBN: 978-1-85345-460-8

The Prodigal Son
Amazing grace
ISBN: 978-1-85345-412-7

The Second Coming
Living in the light of Jesus' return
ISBN: 978-1-85345-422-6

The Sermon on the Mount
Life within the new covenant
ISBN: 978-1-85345-370-0

The Tabernacle
Entering into God's presence
ISBN: 978-1-85345-230-7

The Ten Commandments
Living God's Way
ISBN: 978-1-85345-593-3

The Uniqueness of our Faith
What makes Christianity distinctive?
ISBN: 978-1-85345-232-1

For current prices or to order visit www.cwr.org.uk/store
Available online or from a Christian bookshop.

Cover to Cover Every Day
Gain deeper knowledge of the Bible

Each issue of these bimonthly daily Bible-reading notes gives you insightful commentary on a book of the Old and New Testaments with reflections on a psalm each weekend by Philip Greenslade.

Enjoy contributions from two well-known authors every two months and over a five-year period you will be taken through the entire Bible.

Only £2.95 each (plus p&p)
£15.95 for UK annual subscription (bimonthly, p&p included)
£14.25 for annual email subscription
(available from www.cwr.org.uk/store)

 Individual issues available in epub/Kindle formats

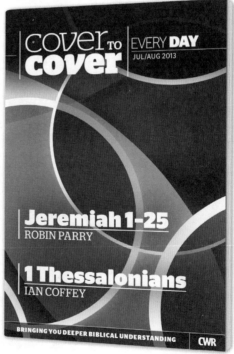

Prices correct at time of printing
To order visit www.cwr.org.uk/store
Available online or from Christian bookshops.

Cover to Cover Complete - NIV Edition
Read through the Bible chronologically

Take an exciting, year-long journey through the Bible, following events as they happened.

- See God's strategic plan of redemption unfold across the centuries
- Increase your confidence in the Bible as God's inspired message
- Come to know your heavenly Father in a deeper way

The full text of the NIV provides an exhilarating reading experience and is augmented by our beautiful:

- Illustrations
- Maps
- Charts
- Diagrams
- Timeline

And key Scripture verses and devotional thoughts make each day's reading more meaningful.

ISBN: 978-1-85345-804-0

For current price or to order visit www.cwr.org.uk/store
Available online or from Christian bookshops.